Disney Princess

Princess

Summer Annual

Once upon a time, in fairy-tale kingdoms far away, there lived five beautiful princesses.

Contents

EGMONT

We bring stories to life

First published in Great Britain in 2009 by Egmont UK Limited,
239 Kensington High Street, London W8 6SA.

Editor: Sally Gilbert
Designer: Laura Bird
Photography: Laura Ashman

ISBN 978 1 4052 4517 3
1 3 5 7 9 10 8 6 4 2
Printed in Italy.

Note to parents: adult supervision is recommended when sharp-pointed items such as scissors are in use.

Turn the page to begin the fairy-tale ...

Ariel

Summer Factfile

- My name is Ariel and I am a mermaid princess. I love having fun and going on adventures with my friends.
- I like picking sea-flowers in summertime.
- I enjoy watching humans have fun on their summer holidays.

Summer Holiday

1

One day, Ariel and Sebastian were watching the world of humans. "Those children are on holiday," Sebastian told Ariel. "It looks such fun," Ariel replied.

2

Later, as Ariel and Sebastian swam down to the Underwater Kingdom again, Ariel had an idea. "It would be great if we could all go on holiday, too!" she thought.

3

So Ariel swam to ask her father, King Triton, if the royal family could go on holiday. "I'm afraid I am far too busy to leave the Underwater Kingdom!" King Triton said.

4

Ariel thought it was a shame that her father was too busy to go on holiday, so she came up with an idea.

5

She asked the royal architect to create a holiday villa right next to the palace, so her father could still watch over the kingdom. "I think this is a great idea, Ariel," King Triton said.

6

"And here's an area of unused land where we can build the villa. It's right next to the palace," King Triton continued.

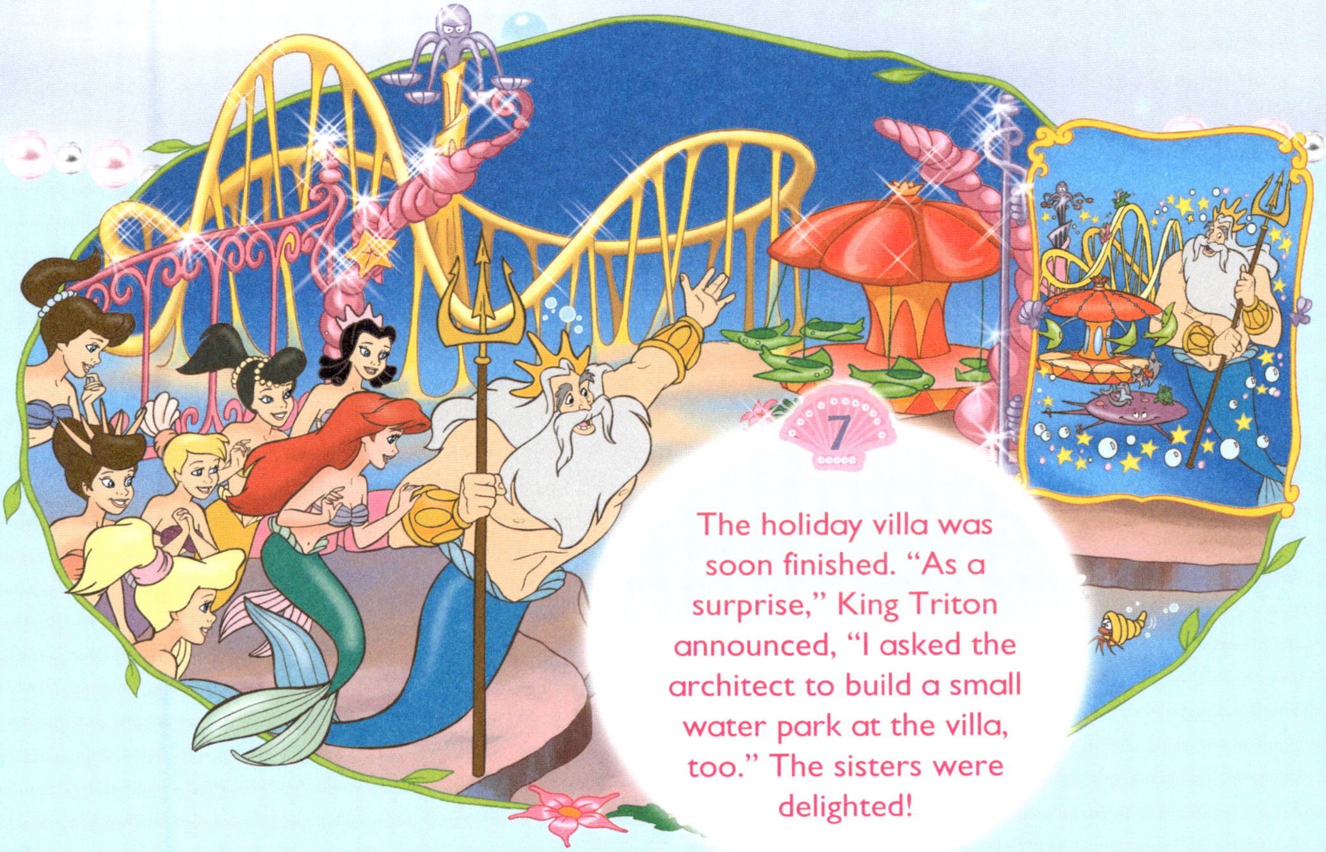

7

The holiday villa was soon finished. "As a surprise," King Triton announced, "I asked the architect to build a small water park at the villa, too." The sisters were delighted!

8

The night before the holiday, King Triton said to Ariel, "Thank you for making me see that everyone needs a holiday...even kings!"

9

On the first day of the holiday, once they had unpacked their suitcases, they relaxed and had fun around the swimming pool.

10

Ariel even showed her sisters how to make a sandcastle, just like the one she had seen the children make in the human world.

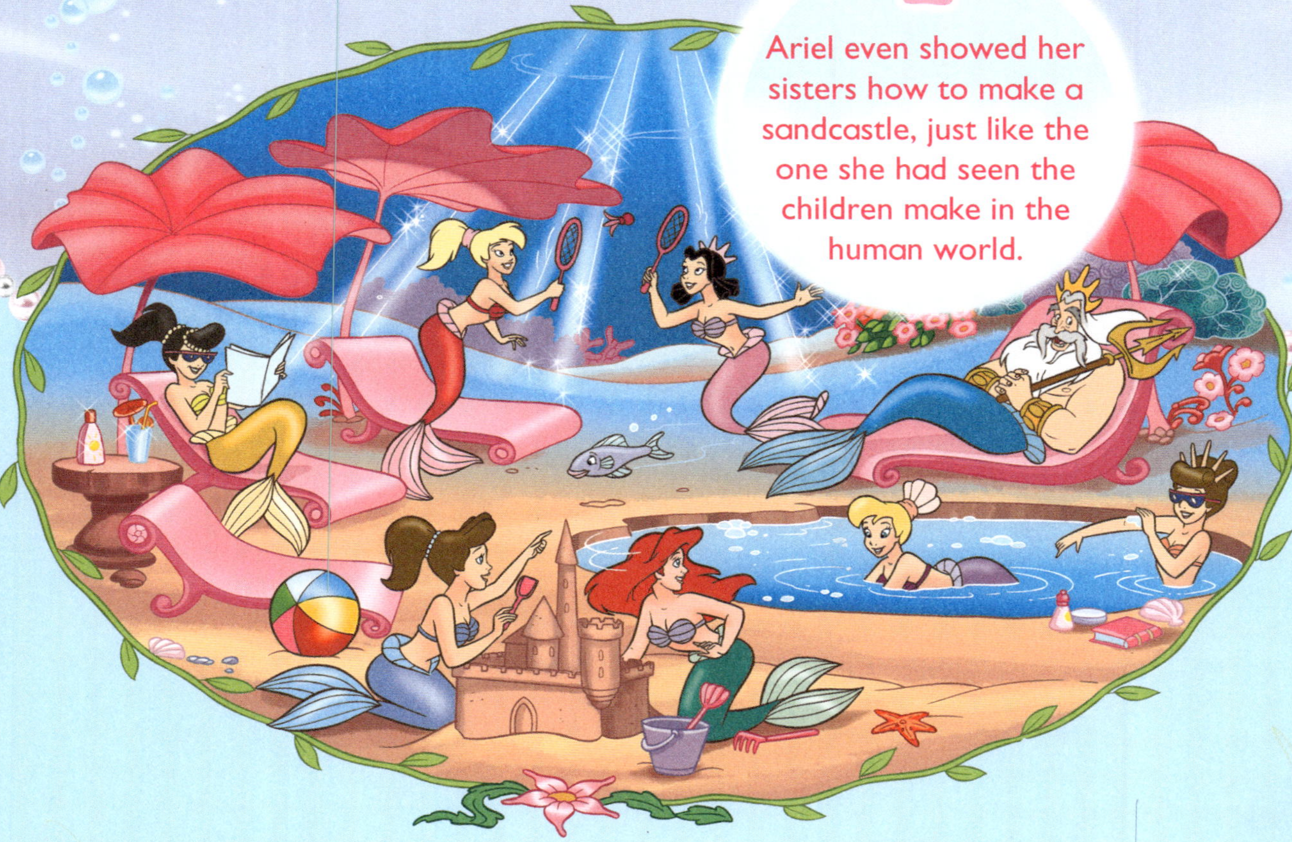

11

"It looks like this holiday lark is catching," said Ariel, as she pointed to Ursula enjoying her own little holiday. "Here's to the next holiday," said King Triton. "I can't wait!"

The End

Finish colouring in this pretty picture of Ariel and then add some stickers.

Sea Sunglasses

Make and wear Ariel's sea-flower sunglasses!

You will need:

cotton material

sunglasses

jewels

scissors

glue

1 To make each sea-flower, ask an adult to help you cut out two flower shapes from the material and neatly glue them on top of each other.

2 Stick a jewel in the middle of each flower. Glue the flowers on to the sunglasses. Wear your pretty sea sunglasses on a sunny day!

Sea Changes

Ariel is playing on her sea-swing.

These pictures look the same but there are 5 changes in picture 2.
Place a sticker on a shell shape each time you spot one.

1

2

Answers: a fish has changed colour, a sea-snail has disappeared, a flower has changed colour, a sea-flower has vanished, a giant bubble has appeared.

Belle

Summer Factfile

- My name is Belle and I live at the Beast's castle. I am a loyal and kind friend.
- I like summer because I see lots of pretty butterflies.
- The summer flowers in the Beast's garden are beautiful.

Petal Power

The Beast has given Belle one of these bouquets.

Follow the ribbons to find out which one it is.

Answer: bouquet c.

Finish colouring in this picture of Belle and then add some stickers.

Seaside Fun

Belle and the Beast are enjoying a summer's day.

Look at the scene below and decide if what Belle is saying is True or False by placing a tick in the correct heart.

2 There is a sandcastle.

True ♡
False ♡

1 Chip is next to the boat.

True ♡
False ♡

Answers: 1-True. 2-True.

Rose Crown

Belle loves this rose crown and so will you.

You will need:

pink card

glue

scissors

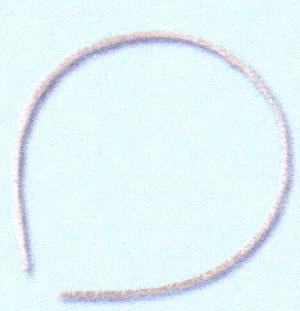

hairband

fabric roses

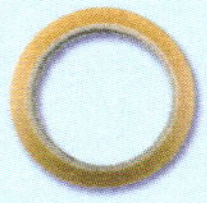

tape

1 Draw a crown shape, as shown, on to the pink card. Ask an adult to help you cut it out. Decorate the crown by sticking on pretty fabric roses.

2 Bend the crown into shape and hold in place with a piece of tape. Tape the crown on to a hairband. Your rose crown is now ready to wear!

Princess Tip:

Why not add stickers, glitter glue and beads to the crown, too?

Cinderella

Summer Factfile

- My name is Cinderella. I am cheerful, good-natured and caring.
- Shawls, parasols and fans are my favourite summer accessories.
- I always look forward to summer balls at the palace.

Summer Surprises

1

One hot summer's morning, Cinderella awoke to find that the Prince had left a present and note on her bed. He had gone on royal business but would return later for a day full of summer surprises!

2

Inside the gift box was a beautiful parasol. Cinderella met the King in the garden, as she went for a stroll.

3

"Good morning, Cinderella. The Prince has a surprise for you," said the King. "Go down to the old oak tree and you will see."

4

Cinderella found a beautiful swing on the old oak tree. "This will keep me cool," Cinderella smiled.

5

Later, the Prince's butler found Cinderella and said, "The Prince would like you to meet him by the lake."

6

So Cinderella went and sat by the lake – it was lovely and cool.

7

After a while, the Prince crept up behind her. "Surprise! I hope you liked my special day so far," he said.

8

The royal couple then had a little dance in the garden. "What a lovely surprise," said Cinderella.

9

Next, the Prince took Cinderella for a romantic walk.

10

Finally, he blindfolded Cinderella and led her to the biggest summer surprise of all.

11

He had made them a wonderful boat to have a summer ball on later. He knew how much Cinderella liked to attend grand balls!

12

But that was not all! Once they moored, he attached a little boat, so they could spend some romantic time alone whilst the sun set! "I love surprises," Cinderella smiled, happily.

The End

Finish colouring in this picture of Cinderella and her prince. You can add some stickers, too!

Flutter Hairband

This butterfly hairband is perfect for a Summer Ball.

You will need:

silver card

coloured card

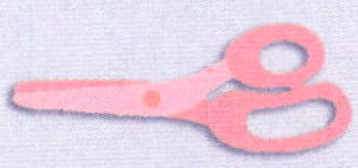

scissors

glue

hairband

1

Draw three butterflies on silver card. Ask an adult to cut out the middle of the wings. Tape coloured paper over the gaps.

2

Glue the butterflies on to a hairband. Your hairband will add the finishing touch to any summer look.

Pretty Fans

Cinderella has lots of pretty fans.

Can you match the pairs and then find the odd one out?

Answers: The pairs are a-h, b-i, c-g, d-f. The odd one out is e.

Snow White

Summer Factfile

- My name is Snow White. I am sweet, generous and trusting.
- I like singing to the birds on a summer's day.
- My prince and I enjoy going on romantic summer picnics together.

Finish colouring in this pretty picture of Snow White
and then add some stickers.

Summer Love

Snow White and her prince are enjoying the sunshine.

Which pieces are missing from the jigsaw picture? Which piece doesn't belong?
Find the stickers and add them to the jigsaw to complete the picture.

Answers: 1-b, 2-d, 3-e, 4-a. c doesn't belong.

Summer Basket

What's inside Snow White's summer basket? Find out in this fun memory game.

How to play

This is a game for one or more players. Study the things in and around Snow White's basket for no longer than one minute. Then cover the picture with a piece of paper and try and remember everything. The player who remembers the most is the winner!

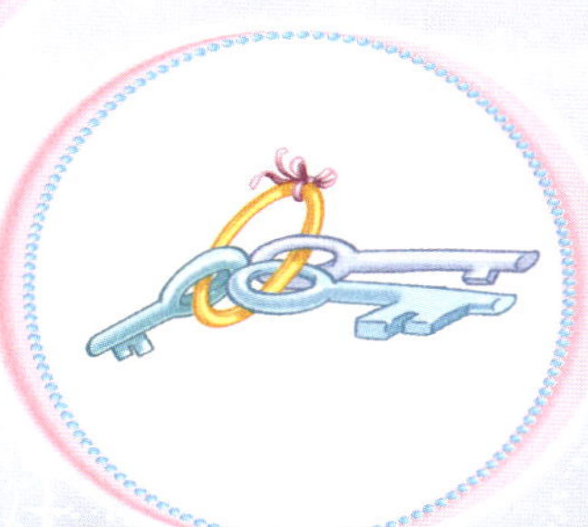

Windmill Fun

This windmill will look pretty blowing in the wind on a summer's day.

You will need:

pink paper

glue

scissors

patterned paper

button

splitpin

straw

Princess Tip:
You could blow the windmill yourself if it's a still day!

1 To make the windmill, ask an adult to help you cut out a square from pretty paper and glue it to a square of plain pink paper. Cut from each corner towards the middle, as shown.

2 Fold the corners into the middle and secure in place with a split pin.

3 Push the split pin through the straw and fasten. Stick a button over the front of the pin to decorate.

Aurora

Summer Factfile

- My name is Aurora. I am romantic, graceful and kind.
- I love wearing summer flowers in my hair.
- My Fairy Godmothers and I like counting butterflies in the woodland.

Summer Returns

1

One summer, the weather had been so bad in Aurora's kingdom that the King called Aurora to his throne room. "I am at my wits' end," he said. "An enchantress has given me this weather bracelet – it is said to only work for a true princess!"

2

Later that day, the King made an announcement: "Aurora is going to bring summer back to this kingdom with this weather bracelet."

3

Aurora put on the bracelet and wished for summer. Of course the weather bracelet worked for her – she was a true princess through and through.

4

The weather soon turned glorious. "Let's have a picnic," Aurora said to the Prince. "There's trouble ahead," the fairies said, "we should follow them and make sure everything is okay!"

5

After the picnic, Aurora and the Prince went boating. "This leaf makes an excellent fan," said Aurora. "It's so hot today!"

6

Everyone had a great time in the sunshine. "I don't want this weather to end," said Aurora.

7

So the next day, Aurora wore the weather bracelet again – the day turned even hotter than before.

8

"We think you should be careful, Aurora with that bracelet – it is dangerous!" said the fairies.

9

Aurora looked around the forest. "I guess my friends do seem a little sleepier than normal," she said, "but maybe they are just tired?"

10

The next day, Aurora wore the bracelet again – and the day was the hottest yet!

11

Later that day, Aurora began to worry. "Oh, dear! The animals look unhappy. Maybe the fairies were right?" she said.

12

When Aurora asked the fairies for their help, the fairies were too tired to even lift their wands. "It's just too hot," Flora yawned.

12

"What shall I do?" Aurora asked the Prince. "I guess there is only one thing you can do," he replied.

13

So Aurora took off the weather bracelet. "I think Mother Nature knows best," said Aurora, as the clouds grew grey. "I hope you know what you are doing, Aurora," warned the King.

14

With the weather bracelet safely packed away, the animals were happy and the fairies could use their magic again. And do you know what? The next day was a perfect summer's day all on its own!

The End

Finish colouring in this picture of Aurora and her Prince. You can add some stickers, too!

All of a Flutter

Can you put the butterflies in order of size, starting with the smallest? Write the answers in the hearts.

Answers: Butterfly c, d, f, a, b, e.

Summer Fun

Test your knowledge of Aurora with this quiz. Match the statements to the correct pictures.

1. What does the Prince pick for me everyday?

2. Which feathered friends do I sing with?

3. Which accessory keeps me cool in the summer?

4. Which friends like gardening?

a

b

c

d

Answers: 1-c. 2-b. 3-d. 4-a.

Flower Hairstyle

Aurora loves wearing flowers in her hair. Now, you can, too.

1 Wash and brush your hair. Put your hair back into a high ponytail.

2 Twist the ponytail into a bun on the top of your head and secure it in place with a hair band and hairgrips.

3

Twist pretty fabric flowers into your hairstyle. You will look like a true summer princess!

Princess Tip:

Ask an adult to curl some front sections of your hair, too.

Jewel Hunt

Play this summer game with your friends and discover who will be crowned the 'Princess of Jewels'.

How to play

You will need: a counter for each player and a dice. You can use your own counters using the stickers. Choose which summer princess you want to be and place your counter on the Start. Take it in turns to throw a dice and move your counter the correct number of spaces along the summer path. If you land on a jewel you can write your initials in your princess's scroll. The first player to claim three jewels is the winner and can write their name on the 'Princess of Jewels' winner's scroll.

The 'Princess of Jewels' is:

....